Comptroller of the Currency
Administrator of National Banks

I0439107

Overview

Comptroller's Handbook

August 1996

CCE

Consumer Compliance Examination

Comptroller's Handbook — Consumer

Since the 1970s, the Office of the Comptroller of the Currency "OCC" has reviewed compliance with various consumer protection laws by national banks, their subsidiaries, federal branches, and federal agencies of foreign banks. Passage of the Truth in Lending Act in 1968 started the age of consumerism. Since that time several consumer protection laws, anti-money laundering laws, fair lending laws, and their implementing regulations have been added. Several of these are part of the Consumer Credit Protection Act, and collectively they are referred to throughout the Comptroller's Handbook — Consumer Compliance Examination as consumer protection laws. A list is provided in the appendix.

The OCC has established a cadre of national bank examiners who devote most of their time to consumer compliance examinations in banks with the highest risk profiles. In other banks, their expertise is available in a consulting or review capacity, as appropriate, to examiners conducting those examinations. This approach incorporates the knowledge of examiners with extensive safety and soundness experience into the consumer compliance examination arena, allowing a thorough risk assessment of the bank.

The Comptroller's Handbook — Consumer Compliance Examination (Handbook) will replace the Comptroller's Handbook for Compliance and An Examiner's Guide to Consumer Compliance (Guide). As Handbook booklets are published, the corresponding sections of the Comptroller's Handbook for Compliance and the Guide will become obsolete. However, the Community Reinvestment Act (CRA) section of the Guide and Banking Bulletin 92-43 will be relevant until July 1, 1997. The Handbook contains current guidance and procedures for examining a national bank's compliance with various consumer protection laws and regulations.

Examination Approach

The OCC uses two approaches in conducting consumer examinations, **performance-** and **process-oriented** procedures. For small community banks, the OCC defines a minimum core set of procedures. These procedures are transaction-based and focus on the results of operations rather than the methods used to achieve them. Examiners reach conclusions about the quality of risk management based on the results of transaction testing. For large banks, the OCC focuses on the bank's method for identifying, measuring, controlling, and monitoring consumer compliance risks. Examiners evaluate the bank's risk management system and perform limited transaction testing to confirm its reliability.

The minimum core set of procedures for small community banks are the "Community Bank Consumer Compliance" examination procedures and, typically, the "Community Reinvestment Act Examination Procedures" for small banks (although some small banks may choose to be evaluated under a different assessment method). The OCC uses these procedures to examine banks with total assets less than $250 million that have no regional or multinational affiliation. Each consumer protection law or regulation is included in the examination. A bank's supervisory office may expand the procedures in any area (except CRA) if a bank offers more complex or high volume products or presents supervisory concerns due to significant violations. When management is ineffective or the bank has a high-risk profile, the supervisory office will set a more specialized examination strategy focusing on the compliance management system the bank has established.

Consumer examinations of large banks are process-oriented (however, the CRA portion of the examination is performance-oriented). Large banks have total assets of $1 billion or more, or are banks that are part of a multibank holding company which includes at least one national bank with assets of $1 billion or more. In these banks, examiners evaluate the bank's compliance management system. Limited transaction testing supplements the system review. This examination approach focuses on the root cause of systemic problems and allows for early recognition of problems. If flaws exist in management's processes for ensuring compliance, the examiner recommends corrective action.

Each consumer examination of a large bank will include an evaluation of the bank's compliance management system in its entirety, and a more detailed analysis of the system to ensure compliance with the Bank Secrecy Act (BSA), fair lending laws and regulations, and the Flood Disaster Protection Act (FDPA). This more detailed system review includes procedures to evaluate the adequacy and accuracy of the compliance audit for BSA, fair lending, and

FDPA. Independent transaction testing need not be performed in these areas if the compliance audit is comprehensive and reliable. The inclusion of other regulatory areas (e.g., Truth in Lending and Truth in Savings) in the examination scope is based on a risk analysis where areas identified as high risk would be included in the scope of the examination. At least one of the areas selected for review must include transaction testing independent of the bank's compliance audit in order to validate the reliability of the bank's compliance management system. Lastly, examiners will evaluate the bank's CRA performance using either the large bank, strategic plan, or the wholesale/limited-purpose examination procedures. Thus, every compliance examination will include a review of the compliance management system, BSA, fair lending, FDPA, CRA and any other regulation(s) identified as high risk.

For those community banks with assets between $250 million and $1 billion, examiners will choose either the performance- or process-oriented procedures, depending on the bank's structure, the history of the bank's compliance management, and examiner judgment. Bank's with large branch networks or complex organizational structures may be more appropriately evaluated using the process-oriented procedures.

Risk Assessment and Interagency Ratings

Throughout the supervisory process, the OCC assesses and re-evaluates each institution's risk profile. From a supervisory perspective, risk is the potential that events, expected or unexpected, may have an adverse impact on the bank's capital or earnings. The OCC has defined nine categories of risk for bank supervision purposes in the Bank Supervision Process booklet. These risks are: **credit, interest rate, liquidity, price, foreign exchange, transaction, compliance, strategic, and reputation.** These categories are not mutually exclusive, any product or service may expose the bank to multiple risks. For analysis and discussion purposes, however, the OCC identifies and assesses the risks separately. The applicable risks associated with consumer protection laws are compliance, transaction, and reputation risk, as described below.

Compliance Risk

Compliance risk is the risk to earnings or capital arising from violations or nonconformance with laws, rules, regulations, prescribed practices, or ethical standards. The risk also arises in situations where the laws or rules governing certain bank products or activities of the bank's clients may be ambiguous or untested. Compliance risk can expose the bank to potential fines, civil money penalties, payment of damages, and the voiding of contracts. Compliance risk can lead to a diminished reputation, reduced franchise value, limited business opportunities, lessened expansion potential, and lack of contract enforceability.

Compliance risk is the predominant risk facing banks with respect to consumer protection laws. This is particularly evident in the area of the Bank Secrecy Act and fair lending laws, where noncompliance can lead to significant fines and/or civil money penalties. Also, noncompliance with the Truth in Lending Act can cause the bank to reimburse customers due to understated annual percentage rates. The failure to properly implement rate changes on variable rate contracts can also lead to the payment of adjustments to customers. Noncompliance with any of the consumer protection laws can also lead to the imposition of a civil money penalty against the bank and/or its employees. All of the above can have an adverse impact on earnings and capital.

Transaction Risk

Transaction risk is the risk to earnings or capital arising from problems with service or product delivery. This risk is a function of internal controls, information systems, employee integrity, and operating processes. Transaction risk exists in all products and services.

Transaction risk is present in every transaction covered by a consumer protection law. Even the slightest error in processing that transaction can have serious repercussions on the institution.

To illustrate, transaction risk can be seen through incorrect adjustments being made to a consumer's variable-rate contract with the bank when interest rates change. If the adjustments are inconsistent with the contract and adversely affect the consumer, the OCC may direct the bank to correct past entries. This may include payment or adjustment to the customer's account to reflect the proper charges. Past occurrences have shown this can be a significant charge to earnings. Likewise, calculation of understated annual percentage rates has resulted in substantial charges to earnings.

Reputation Risk

Reputation risk is the risk to earnings or capital arising from negative public opinion. This affects the bank's ability to establish new relationships or services, or continue servicing existing relationships. This risk can expose the bank to litigation, financial loss, or damage to its reputation. Reputation risk exposure is present throughout the organization and includes the responsibility to exercise an abundance of caution in dealing with its customers and community. This risk is present in such activities as asset management and agency transactions.

Reputation risk exists with respect to the fair lending laws and the Community Reinvestment Act because the results of OCC examinations of these areas are made public through the CRA performance evaluation. The negative publicity that can result from adverse findings can have a significant impact on a bank's reputation in its community. Adverse publicity regarding noncompliance with other laws, such as the Bank Secrecy Act, can also have an adverse impact on a bank's reputation.

Risk Assessment

With respect to the supervision of large bank consumer compliance activities, examiners must evaluate the quantity of compliance and transaction risks, the quality of the management of those risks, the aggregate level of supervisory concern for compliance, transaction and reputation risks, and the direction of compliance, transaction, and reputation risk over the next 12 months. For community banks (those with assets less than $1 billion), examiners must consider the aggregate level of risk and the direction of risk for the three applicable areas (compliance, transaction, and reputation). Guidance is provided in the "Large Bank Supervision" and the "Community Bank Risk Assessment System" booklets on how to measure these risks.

Interagency Ratings

Examiners will continue to assign a composite rating for the institution's consumer and CRA performance using interagency rating definitions as detailed in the appendix of this booklet, the CRA section of An Examiner's Guide to Consumer Compliance, and The Comptroller's Handbook booklet, "Community Reinvestment Act Examination Procedures."

Examination Frequency

In large banks, consumer compliance examinations are conducted on a two-year cycle. Community bank consumer compliance examinations were historically performed based on a random sample of banks each year. Between 1994 and year-end 1996, all community banks will have received a consumer compliance examination. Beginning in January 1997, consumer compliance examinations will occur every 24 or 36 months, based on the safety and soundness examination cycle. Community banks on a 12-month examination cycle will receive a compliance examination at least every 24 months. Community banks on an 18-month examination cycle will receive a compliance examination at least every 36 months. During the safety and soundness examination that occurs in the interval, examiners must at least follow-up on concerns noted at the prior compliance examination. More frequent examinations of CRA may be required if the CRA rating is more than 24 months old and a formal protest from the public is received regarding a corporate application.

Handbook Organization

When conducting a consumer compliance examination, examiners will use appropriate sections of the Comptroller's Handbook – Consumer Compliance Examination, which includes the following sections:

- Overview
- Compliance Management System
- Community Bank Procedures
- Fair Lending
- Flood Disaster Protection
- Bank Secrecy
- Community Reinvestment
  Small Bank
  Large Bank
  Limited Purpose/Wholesale
  Strategic Plan
- Home Mortgage Disclosure
- Real Estate Settlement Procedures
- Fair Credit Reporting

- Truth in Lending
- Depository Services
  Expedited Funds
  Truth in Savings
  Electronic Fund Transfer
  Reserve Requirements
  Interest on Deposits
- Other Consumer Protection Laws and Regulations
  Right to Financial Privacy
  Credit Practices Rule
  Interest on Loans
  Branch Closing Requirements
  Fair Debt Collection
  Consumer Leasing

Examiners also will use several other sections of the Comptroller's Handbook, as described below (all are in the process of being revised or developed, except "Bank Supervision Process" and the "Examination Management Guidebook" which were recently issued). For example, "Examination Planning and Control" procedures must be completed in stand-alone compliance examinations. "Internal and External Audit" procedures must be performed for the bank's compliance audit/review function either by the compliance examiner or by the safety and soundness examiner. Other sections include:

"Bank Supervision Process" — Discusses OCC examination supervision by risk approach and examination frequency and scope requirements.

"Communications" — Details minimum communication requirements (pre-examination communications, board and exit meetings, and reports of examination).

"Examination Planning and Control" — Provides guidance and examination procedures on planning examination activities.

"Internal and External Audits" — Includes guidance and procedures for examining the bank's audit function.

"Internal Control" — Defines internal control and provides guidance on evaluating a bank's internal controls.

"Sampling Methodologies" — Details acceptable sampling methods for OCC examination activities. Specific sampling guidance is provided in other booklets as well. For example, the Fair Lending and Community Bank Consumer Compliance Examination Procedures booklets contain sampling guidelines specific to those areas.

Examination Management Guidebook — Includes request letters for all examination areas, as well as other OCC forms.

The revised Comptroller's Handbook is being issued as a series of booklets so that materials can be kept more current. Each booklet's cover will clearly identify the subject(s) covered and will contain an effective date.

Examiners should discuss booklet contents with bank personnel and welcome suggestions for improvement. All comments, questions, and suggestions are appreciated. Correspondence concerning the Comptroller's Handbook — Consumer Compliance Examination should be addressed to:

> Deputy Comptroller for Compliance Management
> Office of the Comptroller of the Currency
> Washington, DC 20219

Questions about material in the booklets may also be directed to the Compliance Management Division at (202) 874-4428. Calls will be directed to subject matter experts in the specific examination areas. Examiners may send E-mail comments to the OCC.ConsumerHandbook conference board and others may direct comments to the internet address: Consumer.Handbook@OCC.Treas.Gov.

Uniform Interagency Consumer Compliance Rating System

At the recommendation of the Federal Financial Institutions Examination Council, the banking regulatory agencies have adopted the Uniform Interagency Consumer Compliance Rating System. This five-category, numerical rating system standardizes individual agency approaches to measuring the compliance of financial institutions with consumer protection and civil rights laws.

The rating system reflects in a comprehensive and uniform fashion the bank's compliance with consumer protection and civil rights statutes and regulations. The system identifies:

- Banks in need of special supervisory attention.

- The nature and extent of present compliance with consumer protection and civil rights statutes and regulations.

- The commitment of management to compliance and its ability and willingness to assure continuing compliance.

- The adequacy of operating systems, including internal procedures, controls, and audit activities designed to ensure compliance on a routine and consistent basis.

The deputy comptroller or designee must assign a rating based on information in the report of examination. Therefore, the consumer examiner and the reviewing examiner-in-charge (EIC) must ensure that the report includes the information needed to determine a proper compliance rating.

The rating system provides a general framework for evaluating and integrating significant compliance factors to assign a consumer compliance rating to each federally regulated commercial bank, savings and loan association, mutual savings bank, and credit union. The rating system does not consider a bank's record of lending performance under the CRA or its compliance with the applicable provisions of the implementing regulations. Compliance with the Community Reinvestment Act is rated separately.

Overview

Under the uniform rating system, each bank is assigned a consumer compliance rating based on an evaluation of its present compliance with consumer protection and civil rights statutes and regulations and the adequacy of its operating systems designed to ensure continuing compliance. Ratings are given on a scale of 1 through 5 in increasing order of supervisory concern. Thus, 1 represents the highest rating and consequently the lowest level of supervisory concern; while 5 represents the lowest, most critically deficient level of performance and, therefore, the highest degree of supervisory concern.

In assigning a consumer compliance rating, all relevant factors must be evaluated. In general, those factors include:

- The nature and extent of present compliance with consumer protection and civil rights statutes and regulations.

- The commitment of management to compliance and its ability and willingness to assure continuing compliance.

- The adequacy of operating systems, including internal procedures, controls, and audit activities designed to ensure compliance on a routine and consistent basis.

The assignment of a compliance rating may incorporate other factors that significantly affect the overall effectiveness of a bank's compliance efforts.

Although each type of bank differs in its general business powers and constraints, all are subject to the same consumer protection and civil rights laws and regulations covered by the rating system. Thus, there is no need to evaluate differing types of banks on criteria relating to their particular industry. As a result, the assignment of a uniform consumer compliance rating will help direct consistent supervisory attention that does not depend solely upon the nature of the institution's charter or business or the identity of its primary federal regulator. In this manner, overall uniformity and consistency of supervision will be strengthened by the existence of common consumer compliance ratings.

The uniform rating system is intended to help identify those banks whose compliance with consumer protection and civil rights laws and regulations show weaknesses requiring special supervisory attention and which are cause for more than a normal degree of supervisory concern. To accomplish that objective, the rating system identifies an initial category of banks that have compliance deficiencies that warrant more than normal supervisory concern. Those banks are not deemed to present a significant risk of financial or other harm to consumers, but do require a higher than normal level of supervisory attention. Banks in this category are generally rated 3. The rating system also identifies certain banks whose weaknesses are so severe as to represent, in essence, a substantial or general disregard for the law. Those banks, depending upon the nature and degree of their weaknesses, are rated 4 or 5.

Uniformly identifying banks that give cause for more than a normal degree of supervisory concern will help ensure:

• That the degree of supervisory attention and the type of supervisory response are based upon the severity and nature of the bank's problems.

• That supervisory attention and action are, to the extent possible, administered uniformly and consistently, regardless of the type of bank or the identity of the regulatory agency.

• That appropriate supervisory action is taken for those banks whose compliance problems entail the greatest potential for financial or other harm to consumers.

Consumer Compliance Ratings

Consumer compliance ratings are defined as follows:

One: A bank in this category is in a strong compliance position. Management is capable of and staff is sufficient for effectuating compliance. An effective compliance program, including an efficient system of internal procedures and controls, has been established. Changes in consumer statutes and regulations are reflected promptly in the bank's policies, procedures, and compliance training. The bank provides adequate training for its employees. If any violations are noted, they relate to relatively minor deficiencies in forms or practices that are easily corrected. There is no evidence of discriminatory acts or practices, reimbursable violations, or practices resulting in repeat violations. Violations and deficiencies are promptly corrected by management. As a result, the bank gives no cause for supervisory concern.

Two: A bank in this category is in a generally strong compliance position. Management is capable of administering an effective compliance program. Although a system of internal operating procedures and controls has been established to ensure compliance, violations have nonetheless occurred. Those violations, however, involve technical aspects of the law or result from oversight on the part of operating personnel. Modifying the bank's compliance program and/or establishing additional review/audit procedures may eliminate many of the violations. Compliance training is satisfactory. There is no evidence of discriminatory acts or practices, reimbursable violations, or practices resulting in repeat violations.

Three: Generally, a bank in this category is in a less than satisfactory compliance position. It is a cause for supervisory concern and requires more than normal supervision to remedy deficiencies. Violations may be numerous. In addition, previously identified practices resulting in violations may remain uncorrected. Overcharges, if present, involve a few consumers and are minimal in amount. There is no evidence of discriminatory acts or practices. Although management may have the ability to effectuate compliance, increased efforts are necessary. The numerous violations discovered indicate that management has not devoted sufficient time and attention to consumer compliance. Operating procedures and controls have not proven effective and require strengthening by, among other things, designating a compliance officer and developing and implementing a comprehensive and effective compliance program. By identifying such a bank early, additional supervisory measures may be employed to eliminate violations and prevent further deterioration in the bank's less than satisfactory compliance position.

Four: A bank in this category requires close supervisory attention and monitoring to correct promptly the serious compliance problems disclosed. Numerous violations are present. Overcharges, if any, affect a significant number of consumers and involve a substantial amount of money. Often practices resulting in violations and cited at previous examinations remain uncorrected. Discriminatory acts or practices may be in evidence. Clearly, management has not exerted sufficient effort to ensure compliance. Its attitude may indicate a lack of interest in administering an effective compliance program that may have contributed to the seriousness of the bank's compliance problems. Internal procedures and controls have not proven effective and are seriously deficient. Prompt action on the part of the supervisory agency may enable the bank to correct its deficiencies and improve its compliance position.

Five: A bank in this category needs the strongest supervisory attention and monitoring. It is substantially in noncompliance with the consumer laws and regulations. Management has demonstrated its unwillingness or inability to operate within the scope of consumer laws and regulations. Previous efforts on the part of the regulatory authority to obtain voluntary compliance have been unproductive. Discrimination, substantial overcharges, or practices resulting in serious repeat violations are present.

Consumer Protection Laws and Regulations

Since the 1970s the OCC has enforced the various consumer protection laws in national banks, their subsidiaries, federal branches, and federal agencies of foreign banks. Passage of the Truth in Lending Act in 1968 started an era of consumerism. Since that time, a number of consumer protection laws, anti-money laundering laws, fair lending laws and their implementing regulations have been added. Several of these are part of the Consumer Credit Protection Act, and collectively they are referred to throughout the Comptroller's Handbook — Consumer as consumer protection laws. Here is a summary of the consumer protection laws that are part of the OCC's consumer compliance examination:

Consumer Credit Protection Act

Congress enacted the Consumer Credit Protection Act (CCPA) on May 29, 1968. The law incorporates seven major pieces of legislation, each of which is known separately by its descriptive title. The parts of the CCPA are:

- Truth in Lending Act (TILA). Title I, Chapters 1-3 of the CCPA. Truth in Lending was the only matter considered when the CCPA was enacted. The act was implemented by Regulation Z of the Federal Reserve Board, which became effective July 1, 1969.

- Fair Credit Billing Act (FCBA). Title I, Chapter 4 of the CCPA. The act, effective on October 28, 1975, was implemented by Regulation Z of the Federal Reserve Board.

- Consumer Leasing Act of 1976. Title I, Chapter 5 of the CCPA. The act, effective March 23, 1977, was implemented by Regulation M of the Federal Reserve Board.

- Fair Credit Reporting Act (FCRA). Title VI of the CCPA. The act became effective on April 25, 1971. There are no regulations to implement the FCRA although the Federal Trade Commission (FTC) is authorized to issue interpretations of the act.

- Equal Credit Opportunity Act (ECOA). Title VII of the CCPA. The act, effective October 28, 1975, was implemented by Regulation B of the Federal Reserve Board.

- Fair Debt Collection Practices Act (FDCPA). Title VIII of the CCPA. The Act became effective March 20, 1978. There are no implementing regulations. The FTC is authorized to issue advisory opinions.

- Electronic Fund Transfers Act (EFTA). Title IX of the CCPA. The act, effective May 10, 1980, was implemented by Regulation E of the Federal Reserve Board.

Other Consumer Protection Laws

In addition to the Consumer Credit Protection Act, several other laws and regulations are included in the OCC's review. The following table shows these laws along with those contained in the CCPA, the implementing regulations, and the governmental agency responsible for issuing and updating the regulation.

Table of Laws and Regulations
Consumer Protection Laws

Act or Subject	Statute	Regulation	Agency
Interest Charged -- Usury	12 USC 85, 86a		
Payment of Interest on Demand Deposits	12 USC 371a	12 CFR 217	FRB (Reg. Q)
Mortgages (Usury Preemption)	12 USC 1735f-7	12 CFR 590	OTS
Advertising of FDIC Membership	12 USC 1828(a)	12 CFR 328	FDIC
Consumer Checking Account Equity Act (NOW Accounts)	12 USC 1832	12 CFR 204	FRB (Reg. D)
Real Estate Settlement Procedures Act	12 USC 2601	24 CFR 3500	HUD (Reg. X)
Home Mortgage Disclosure Act	12 USC 2801	12 CFR 203	FRB (Reg. C)
Community Reinvestment Act	12 USC 2901	12 CFR 25	OCC
Right to Financial Privacy Act	12 USC 3401		
Expedited Funds Availability Act	12 USC 4001	12 CFR 229	FRB (Reg. CC)
Truth in Savings Act	12 USC 4301	12 CFR 230	FRB (Reg. DD)
Unfair or Deceptive Acts or Practices	15 USC 57f	12 CFR 227	FRB (Reg. AA)
Truth in Lending Act	15 USC 1601	12 CFR 226	FRB (Reg. Z)
Fair Credit Billing Act	15 USC 1666	12 CFR 226	FRB (Reg. Z)
Consumer Leasing Act	15 USC 1667	12 CFR 213	FRB (Reg. M)
Fair Credit Reporting Act	15 USC 1681		
Equal Credit Opportunity Act	15 USC 1691	12 CFR 202	FRB (Reg. B)
Fair Debt Collection Practices Act	15 USC 1692		
Electronic Funds Transfer Act	15 USC 1693	12 CFR 205	FRB (Reg. E)
Bank Secrecy Act	31 USC 3334	12 CFR 21	OCC
		31 CFR 103	US Treasury
Fair Housing Act	42 USC 3601	24 CFR 100	HUD
Flood Disaster Protection Act	42 USC 4002	12 CFR 22	OCC
Fair Housing Home Loan Data System		12 CFR 27	OCC
Real Estate Loans		12 CFR 34	OCC
(Adjustable-rate Mortgages)		12 CFR 226	FRB (Reg. Z)

Violations of Law and Regulation

Only significant violations should be included in the report of examination (ROE). Significant violations include, but are not limited to, those that involve criminal penalties, reimbursement, referral to other agencies, or a significant risk to the bank's capital, earnings or reputation, or violations that are subject to an OCC or interagency policy guide. Depending on the facts and circumstances, repeat violations or violations indicating a pattern or practice may represent significant violations. Technical violations that are individually insignificant, but that collectively indicate system weaknesses may be reflected in the ROE as a listing of violation cites (no write-ups). All violations must be recorded in SMS and presented to management, with documentation retained in the work papers.

When evaluating whether violations represent a pattern or practice, examiners must analyze the pertinent facts and circumstances. Isolated, unrelated or accidental occurrences will not constitute a pattern or practice. However, repeated, intentional, regular, usual, deliberate, or institutionalized practices will almost always constitute a pattern or practice. The totality of the circumstances must be considered when assessing whether a pattern or practice is present. Considerations include, but are not limited to:

- Whether the conduct appears to be grounded in a written or unwritten policy or established practice.

- Whether there is evidence of similar conduct by the bank in more than one transaction. However, this is not a mathematical process, i.e., more than one does not necessarily constitute a pattern or practice.

- Whether there is a common source or cause within the bank's control.

- The relationship of the instances of noncompliance to one another (i.e., whether they all occurred in the same area of the bank, in the same product line, or by one employee).

- The relationship of the number of instances of noncompliance to the bank's total activity. However, depending on the circumstances, violations that involve only a small percentage of a bank's total activity could constitute a pattern or practice.

Depending on the egregiousness of the facts and circumstances involved, singly or in combination, these factors could provide evidence of a pattern or practice.

Applicability to Trust Departments

The following excerpt of an interpretive letter was issued by the OCC on the applicability of seven consumer protection laws, including fair lending laws to national banks' trust departments:

Equal Credit Opportunity Act

The Equal Credit Opportunity Act (ECOA), 15 USC 1691, is intended to prevent creditors from discriminating against applicants for credit (1) on the basis of race, color, religion, national origin, sex, marital status, or age, (2) because the applicant receives income from public assistance programs, or (3) because of the applicant's good faith exercise of any right under the Consumer Credit Protection Act. The ECOA is implemented by the Federal Reserve Board's (FRBs) Regulation B and applies to any creditor, which is defined to include "a person who, in the ordinary course of business, regularly participates in the decision of whether or not to extend credit." 12 CFR 202.2(1). The bank inquires whether the person referenced would be the bank acting as trustee or the individual trust in a transaction involving a decision whether or not to extend credit from the trust.

Your letter indicates that FRB staff has informally advised the bank that the person in such transactions would be the individual trust and not a bank as trustee. Even though a bank as trustee literally "participates in the decision whether or not to extend credit," the staff position is that the trustee acts as an agent or employee of the trust and that the trustee is therefore identified with the trust for purposes of Regulation B. Accordingly, under this interpretation which we have informally confirmed with the FRB staff, the business of the trust itself rather than the collective business of the bank trustee should be evaluated to determine whether Regulation B applies.

The bank also seeks guidance on which agency should be disclosed to applicants as having authority to administer compliance with the ECOA, when an individual trust is a creditor under the act. The ECOA provides that the OCC has enforcement authority in the case of national banks and that the Federal Trade Commission (FTC) has enforcement authority in any case for which another governmental agency is not specifically granted enforcement authority. See ECOA, Section 704(a) and (c). Thus, the issue is whether the OCC or the FTC has enforcement authority when the creditor is an individual trust which has a national bank as trustee.

Because the trustee is the entity with discretion to make credit decisions on behalf of an individual trust, the trustee will be responsible for the trust's compliance with ECOA. As trustee, the national bank also would be required to defend the trust in the event of an enforcement action brought under the ECOA. Given that the trustee has these substantive functions with respect to the ECOA, it is logical that the OCC, the agency charged with enforcing the ECOA in the case of national banks, should have jurisdiction over national banks acting as trustee for trusts that are subject to the ECOA. Therefore, the OCC would expect to be named as the agency with enforcement authority for cases involving national bank trustees. As this question has not been decided by any court, you also may wish to consult with the FTC.

Fair Housing Act

The Fair Housing Act (FHA), 42 USC 3601, prohibits discrimination in all aspects of the sale, financing, or rental of housing, on the basis of race, color, religion, sex, handicap, familial status or national origin. The FHA is a broad, remedial statute intended to implement "the policy of the United States to provide, within constitutional limitations, for fair housing throughout the United States." FHA, Section 801.

The bank questions the extent to which the FHA applies to trust department activities that involve (1) the sale or rental of trust assets consisting of residential property, and (2) extensions of credit from trust funds for purposes of financing residential housing. The bank also inquires whether the Fair Housing Poster required to be displayed under the Department of Housing and Urban Development's (HUDs) implementing regulations must be posted in the trust department. As discussed below, it is our conclusion that the prohibitions contained in the FHA apply to a bank acting as trustee regardless of whether the individual trust involved would be subject to the act. Also depending on its activities, we conclude that an individual trust also might be subject to the act.

Discrimination in Sale or Rental. Section 804 of the FHA broadly states that "it shall be unlawful" to discriminate in the sale or rental of housing or to engage in other specified discriminatory housing practices. The exception that could apply to the bank's inquiry is contained in Section 803(b). This section provides an exception from Section 804 for any single family house sold or rented by a private individual owner who does not own or have any interest in more than three such houses at one time, provided that (1) the exception applies only once within any two-year period if the owner did not reside in the house or was not its most recent occupant at the time of disposition; and (2) the house may not be sold or rented using the services of any real estate broker, agent, salesman, or the facilities of any person in the business of selling or renting dwellings.

The bank questions whether Section 804 applies to the bank itself, acting as trustee, or whether each trust must be considered separately under this section. The OCC has historically interpreted Section 804 as applying to national banks acting as trustees. Assuming that Section 804 applies to the bank as trustee, it also seems clear that the exception provided in Section 803 would not be available. A national bank trustee would not be a "private individual owner" capable of residing in the dwelling, and the bank as trustee would be likely to own (have legal title to) more than three single-family houses.

Because Section 804 is so broadly worded, we conclude that its prohibitions would also apply separately to each individual trust. Although the statute is not explicit, the use of the words "private individual owner" and the reference to the owner's residence indicate that the exception is intended for natural persons. Also, any sale or rental of trust property would necessarily involve using the services of the trustee. As noted above, Section 803 exempts only transactions that are effected without the use of a "real estate broker or agent . . . ." The terms broker and agent are broadly defined in HUD's regulation to include any person "authorized to perform an action on behalf of another person regarding any matter related to the sale or rental of dwellings . . . including offers, solicitations or contracts and the administration [thereof] . . . ." 24 CFR 100.20. In view of the expansiveness of this definition, it appears that the use of the trustee's services in selling or renting the trust property would constitute the use of a real estate broker or agent and would therefore render the exemption unavailable for the trust.

Discrimination in Financing. Section 805 of the FHA provides that "it shall be unlawful for any person or other entity whose business includes engaging in residential real estate-related transactions to discriminate . . . in making available such a transaction . . . ." The term "residential real estate-related transaction" is broadly defined to include extensions of credit secured by residential real estate or for the purpose of acquiring or maintaining a dwelling, as well as the selling, brokering, or appraising of residential property. The bank inquires whether the collective activities of the national bank as trustee or the separate activities of each individual trust should be evaluated in determining the application of this section.

As with Section 804, Section 805 establishes a broad prohibition against discrimination. The section applies to any person whose business includes the described activities. The FHA defines person to include trusts, trustees, and fiduciaries. See FHA, Section 802(d). A national bank as trustee, which would ordinarily have discretion to make lending decisions on behalf of numerous trusts, would be a person that could be engaged in a business that includes residential real estate-related transactions. Additionally, because the FHA definition of a person also includes a trust, it is also possible that Section 805 will apply to an individual trust, based upon the extent of an individual trust's residential real estate activities.

Fair Housing Poster. The bank also inquires whether the fair housing poster required under HUD's regulation, 24 CFR 110, must be posted in the trust department. This regulation applies to all persons subject to Sections 804 through 806 of the FHA.

See 24 CFR 110.1. Depending on where the bank's trust department is located relative to the main lobby (assuming the poster is already posted there), the bank should determine if additional posters are required. For example, if persons entering the trust department to engage in transactions covered by the FHA would not be aware of existing posters, the simple and prudent course would be for the bank to post an additional poster in the trust department. The bank should be aware that in the event of a lawsuit, failure to comply with this regulation will be deemed prima facie evidence of a discriminatory housing practice. See 24 CFR 110.30. (Note: The OCC does not enforce the requirements of 24 CFR 110 with respect to the fair housing poster, however, the OCC does recommend that banks comply with its provisions since a failure to do so will be deemed by HUD prima facie evidence of a discriminatory housing practice in an investigation of a complaint filed against the bank.)

Fair Credit Reporting Act

The bank questions whether the Fair Credit Reporting Act (FCRA) applies if a national bank acting as trustee uses information contained in a consumer report as part of its determination whether to lease trust-owned property to a consumer. The question presented is whether the denial of a lease would constitute the denial of credit for purposes of the FCRA.

The only court to have addressed this matter, to our knowledge, has concluded the FCRAs adverse notification requirements can apply to leasing transactions. See Ferguson v. Park City Mobile Homes, No. 89-C-1909 (N.D. Ill. September 15, 1989). In this case the court first concluded that the ECOA can apply to a lease transaction, based on the broad definition of credit transaction contained in the act. See also Brothers v. First Leasing, 724 F. 2d 789 (9th Cir.), cert. denied, 489 U.S. 832 (1984)). Regarding the FCRA issue, the court stated "[a]s an economic matter, any lease to be paid in installments is a credit transaction, since the willingness of the lessor to defer payments over the life of the lease depends upon the perceived creditworthiness of the leasee." Ferguson. at 5.

Electronic Fund Transfer Act

The Electronic Fund Transfer Act (EFTA), 15 USC 1693, applies to electronic fund transfers to or from consumer accounts. The bank inquires whether the EFTA applies to electronic fund transfers involving trust accounts. We agree with the bank's conclusion that transactions involving trust accounts are not subject to the EFTA. The definition of account contained in Regulation E, the FRBs regulation implementing the EFTA, specifically excludes "an account held by a financial institution pursuant to a bona fide trust agreement." See 12 CFR 205.3(f). See also 12 CFR Part 205, Supp. II, Question 3-20 (discussing custodial agreements).

12 CFR Part 590

Under the Office of Thrift Supervision's regulation at 12 CFR 590, state usury laws are preempted and made inapplicable to federally related loans secured by residential property. The bank inquires whether the lending activities of the trust department as a whole should be evaluated or whether the lending activities of each individual trust should be considered separately to determine this regulation's application. Based upon our reading of the regulation, each trust's loans must be considered separately to determine whether they are subject to 12 CFR 590.

Real Estate Settlement Procedures Act

The Real Estate Settlement Procedures Act (RESPA), 12 USC 2601, requires certain disclosures to borrowers and provides protection against certain abusive practices in connection with the real estate settlement process. The act applies to federally related mortgage loans made by lenders, as defined in HUD's implementing regulation under RESPA, Regulation X. See 24 CFR 3500. To determine whether this act applies to loans made through its trust department, the bank inquires whether the definition of lender should be applied to the trust department as a whole or to the individual trusts. Based upon our review of the act and Regulation X, we conclude that each trust's activities must be considered separately to determine whether RESPA applies to loans funded with trust assets.

Flood Disaster Protection Act of 1973

Under the Flood Disaster Protection Act (FDPA), 42 USC 4002, federal financial institution regulators are directed to issue regulations prohibiting institutions under their jurisdictions from extending credit secured by improved real property in certain areas unless the property has flood hazard insurance. The OCC's implementing regulation under the FDPA is 12 CFR 22. The bank inquires whether loans funded with trust assets and made through a national bank's trust department are subject to the FDPA.

As your letter points out, the OCC's regulations apply to "certain loans secured by improved real estate made by banks . . ." (emphasis added). The term "bank" is defined to mean a national banking association, with no reference to the bank as trustee. Based on this plain language reading of the regulation, and in view of the congressional concern expressed over the extent to which the assets of federally regulated or insured financial institutions consist of loans made in flood hazard areas, we agree that this regulation does not reach loans funded from individual trusts. See 42 USC 4002(a)(4) — Congressional Finding. However, in order for the bank to comply with its fiduciary obligations as trustee, it may still be necessary for the bank to require flood insurance coverage for property that secures loans extended from individual trusts.

Federal Branches and Agencies of Foreign Banks

The OCC is responsible for conducting consumer compliance examinations in federal branches and agencies of foreign banks. The International Banking Act of 1978 (IBA) sets forth the basic framework for the operations of foreign bank offices in the United States. The IBA provides that, unless otherwise provided by law or the OCC, the operations of a foreign bank at its federal branch or agency are conducted with the same liabilities, conditions, and limitations that would be applicable to a national bank operating in the same location as the federal branch or agency, 12 USC 3102(b). The OCC's regulation implementing the IBA, 12 CFR 28, restates this principle. When a federal branch or agency engages in activity that is covered by the applicable consumer protection law or regulation, then it is subject to that law or regulation to the same extent as a national bank, 12 USC 3106a (as amended by section 107(c) of the Riegle-Neal Interstate Banking and Branching Efficiency Act of 1994).

In general, if a particular law or regulation exempts branches or agencies of foreign banks from its provisions, then such exemption is valid and the particular law or regulation will not apply. For example, the OCC's CRA regulations explicitly state that the CRA does not apply to uninsured federal branches and agencies (those that do not accept insured deposits).

Joint Policy Statement on Basic Financial Services

The Office of the Comptroller of the Currency and other financial institution regulators issued the following joint policy statement to encourage trade associations and individual depository institutions regarding basic financial services.

The economic environment in which financial institutions operate has changed over the past few years, due in part to increased competition from outside the traditional depository institution structure, increased cost of funds following deregulation of interest rates, and interest rate volatility. As a consequence, many institutions have had to adopt new strategies to market their services, generate income, manage risk, and reduce costs. Some institutions have begun to price their products explicitly, consolidate or eliminate services they believe to be unprofitable, and close branch offices. In many instances, institutions have increased service charges, imposed new fees, and raised minimum balance requirements.

Although such adaptation may be a necessary response to competitive markets, considerable concern has developed about the potential impact of these changes in effectively denying or reducing convenient access of many individuals to the payments system and to safe depositories for small savings. Because credit availability often depends on an account relationship with a financial institution, access to credit for low-income or young consumers also may be adversely affected.

Although a significant number of consumers have never had a deposit account, some research studies reflect declines in account ownership that may be cause for concern. For example, between 1977 and 1983, the proportion of families headed by a younger person having checking accounts decreased, as did the number of families from the lowest income group, regardless of age. The proportion of young families having either a savings or a checking account also declined. Although the cause of these declines is not always clear, the surveys do suggest that a significant number of individuals or families do not have a deposit relationship of any kind.

Legislation dealing with basic financial services has been introduced at both the federal and state level as a result of these concerns. The industry also has responded. Many financial institutions independently have undertaken to develop and implement new measures to meet minimum consumer needs. They are offering basic services, such as low-cost transaction and savings accounts with low or no minimum balances, accounts for consumers who use a limited number of checks or drafts, and other accounts on which minimal charges are made for account maintenance.

Institutions that have for years offered such services to particular groups of customers are now advertising more widely their availability. Other institutions are exploring and finding ways to maintain a physical presence in low- and moderate-income neighborhoods even while reducing the expense normally associated with full branch facilities. Trade groups too have joined in these efforts to encourage the offering of such services at affordable prices. The American Bankers Association and Consumer Bankers Association, for example, have called on their members to address the continuing interest in basic banking services.

The member agencies of the Federal Financial Institutions Examination Council and the associations of state supervisors wish to encourage such efforts by trade associations and individual depository institutions that promote the offering of basic financial services, consistent with safe and sound business practices. Although the specific type of services will, of course, vary because of differences in local needs and in the characteristics of individual institutions, we encourage efforts to meet certain minimum needs of all consumers, in particular:

- The need for a safe and accessible place to keep money.

- The need for a way to obtain cash (including, for example, the cashing of government checks).

- The need for a way to make third-party payments.

We believe that industry trade associations have a key role to play in this effort and are in a position to encourage a constructive response without the rigidities of legislation or regulation. We realize that some associations have such programs already under way.

These programs could usefully:

- Encourage members to offer and publicize appropriately low-cost basic financial services, such as those listed above.

- Survey the current availability of such services among member institutions.

- Make available to members not providing such services material reflecting the successful experiences of other organizations.

OCC Policy on Basic Banking Services

National banks are encouraged to develop policies and procedures for offering basic banking services at reasonable prices to consumers in their communities. We encourage banks to think creatively about using cost saving mechanisms, such as technology and check truncation, in a way that is sensitive to the needs of consumers of financial services. Additionally, national banks should voluntarily disclose to their communities the availability and terms of these services. The type of services provided should be determined by an assessment of consumer needs in the bank's community.

Consistent with prudent management practices, policies of national banks' covering basic banking services might include consideration of:

- A basic transaction account with no or limited minimum balance requirement and commensurate overdraft charges and related service fees.

- Low-cost or free cashing of government checks (federal, state and local transfer payments).

- Customer access, on a convenient basis, to bank employees for advice and other help related to basic banking services.

- Plain-English, written disclosure of all fees, services, and terms of the basic banking services.

OCC Issuances

Banking Bulletin 92-43, Community Reinvestment Act (CRA) Examination Procedures

An Examiner's Guide to Consumer Compliance
Comptroller's Handbook for Compliance

The Comptroller's Handbook, "Community Reinvestment Act"
The Comptroller's Handbook, "Community Bank Consumer Compliance"
The Comptroller's Handbook, "Bank Supervision Process"
The Comptroller's Handbook, "Large Bank Supervision"
The Comptroller's Handbook, "Community Bank Risk Assessment System"
The Comptroller's Handbook, "Examination Planning and Control"

"Examination Management Guidebook" (Computer-based Guide)